Building Bridges, Scaling Walls

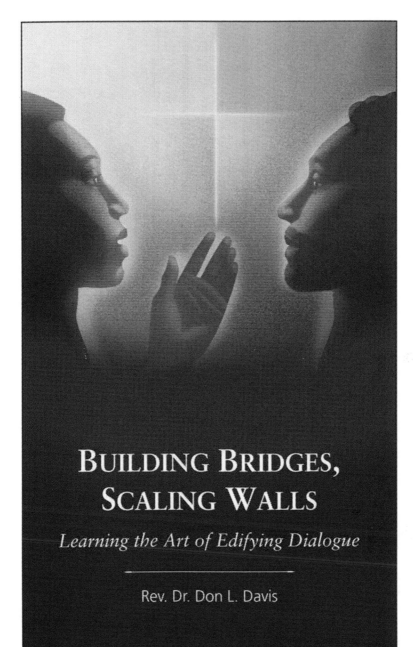

BUILDING BRIDGES, SCALING WALLS

Learning the Art of Edifying Dialogue

Rev. Dr. Don L. Davis

TUMI Press • 3701 East 13th Street North • Wichita, Kansas 67208

I dedicate this book to my colleagues and friends,
TUMI graduates and students scattered around the world –
my wise and fierce dialogue partners committed all
to speaking the truth in love,
to the glory of Jesus of Nazareth.

Table of Contents

Introduction

Every man is a potential adversary, even those whom we love. Only through dialogue are we saved from this enmity toward one another. Dialogue is to love, what blood is to the body. When the flow of blood stops, the body dies. When dialogue stops, love dies and resentment and hate are born. But dialogue can restore a dead relationship. Indeed, this is the miracle of dialogue: it can bring relationship into being, and it can bring into being once again a relationship that has died.

~ Reuel Howe, *The Miracle of Dialogue.*
New York: The Seabury Press, 1963. p. 3.

This booklet deals briefly with the subject of dialogue, describing its nature through a discussion of ten principles related to mature communication. The entire idea of building bridges instead of erecting walls – that is my hope in penning this little book. In the wake of so many difficult, thorny, and intractable issues being discussed and debated today, the follower of Christ must abide in his word, knowing the truth that sets free (John 8.31-32). Add to this too, the word "art" in the title. This term highlights the learned quality of the dialogue skill. It demands constant practice, adjustment, learning, and craft. The more one engages in the process of dialogue, the better one learns the craft and experiences its unique benefits and blessings.

To offer kingdom witness in this world to our friends and families and to our neighbors and associates, will demand that we learn to dialogue with others whose views will dramatically differ from our own. To be an effective witness today we must learn the arts and skills of a good ambassador (2 Cor. 5.20), able to offer everyone who asks us for a reason for our hope a clear and compelling answer (1 Pet. 3.15-16). I believe that as we study carefully the basic principles of good dialogue, we can become solid witnesses, more convincing in our ideas and arguments, and better able to help others come to understand the truth that we hold so dear.

For the purpose of this little book's organization, I am using a straightforward approach, striving to be as direct and non-technical as possible. This method will prove crucial for my argument's purpose, for several reasons. First, it is critical to know how to relate to others when you are discussing difficult or even "dangerous" issues. Second, as Howe says above, dialogue is to relationship, what blood is to the body – no relationships can be developed or enriched without it. And third, dialogue can transform a toxic communication space only by being built on a basic knowledge of its underlying principles, those truths that enable you to be gracious and clear in interacting with others.

Truly open and honest dialogue is the best way to engage and discover another person's opinion and argument and represents a safe, humane, and nonviolent way to settle disputes, conflicts, and disagreements over tough or unclear issues. Godly, sincere, and open-minded people can and often do disagree on various themes that confront them together. How we choose to handle those disagreements may turn out to be some of the most critical decisions in our entire lives. In my view, the most significant thing that we can do in this regard is to create a process and a way of relating that allows us to handle our disagreements openly and honestly. We must learn to listen carefully to the opinions of others without caricaturing or twisting them, and seek to be open to their alternative views on what we are considering to debate or discuss.

Nothing can be worse in communication and dialogue than thinking that just because you hold your views honestly and with deep feeling that your opinions are somehow automatically accurate and valid. Committed disciples of Jesus may come to disagree about things that all parties involved deeply hold dear. It takes time and effort to understand another person's view and to hear their arguments and evidence without prejudice or bias. Good dialogue is an expression of humility. That dialogue focuses on understanding the other's viewpoint first, even before we make our own opinions known. "But the wisdom from above is first pure, then peaceable, gentle, open to reason, full of mercy and good fruits, impartial and sincere. And a harvest of righteousness is sown in peace by those who make peace" (James 3.17-18).

The structure of this booklet is simple. In general outline, to begin with, I provide an appropriate quote from Howe on dialogue related to the principle. I then discuss each principle briefly, providing practical insight into what it means, and clear advice on how we, as dialogue partners, can make this principle work itself out in our practice and discussions. We will concentrate on what it takes to understand another person first and to see that as a primary value. Only after we have paid the price to understand another should we then seek to be understood. As critical as anything else in human relating, dialogue offers us a clear path to better decisions, clearer truth-seeking, better clarity on the facts, and wiser policies that affect our lives. While understanding such material may be challenging and a little abstract, the time spent thinking these things through can transform our lives. Dialogue, rightly done, leads to the truth, that is, to a deeper understanding of the person and will of the Lord Jesus Christ, whose word is still the truth that sets the heart free. It is with this hope and desire that I pen this little essay. May we all learn what it means to speak the truth in love, and so grow up to be fully mature in the Son of God (Eph. 4.11-15).

Many wonderful colleagues have helped me sharpen my skills of dialogue; these principles have been tried and tested in the heat of conversational exchange. Cathy Allsman, TUMI's Incarceration Specialist and the wife of my colleague Don, is a true friend and fellow soldier in the Gospel. I blame her tenacious insistence for the production of this small booklet. Cathy, over time, lovingly cajoled me to get this done, knowing its importance for our biblical students inside the prison walls. Its final completion is largely due to her gentle yet persistent encouragement.

May those who read this small booklet learn the art and skill of open, effective dialogue and so be better able to know the truth and to be set free (John 8.31-32).

Dr. Don L. Davis
January 23, 2018

Recognize that differences among cultures and backgrounds give rise to differences of viewpoints and opinions.

"You say *to-MAY-toe*, and to me, it's *ta-MAH-toe*."

Dialogue is indispensable also in the search for truth and here, too, it is a worker of miracles. Unfortunately, many people hold and proclaim what they believe to be true in either an opinionated or defensive way. Religious people, for example, sometimes speak the truth they profess monologically, that is, they hold it exclusively and inwardly as if there was no possible relation between what they believe and what others believe, in spite of every indication that separately held truths are often complementary. The monological thinker runs the danger of being prejudiced, intolerant, bigoted, and a persecutor of those who differ from him. The dialogical thinker, on the other hand, is willing to speak out of his convictions to the holders of other convictions with genuine interest in them and with a sense of the possibilities between them.

~ Howe, *ibid.*, pp. 9-10.

In dialogue and communication, we encounter people who are different than we are – in history, in personal life journeys, and perspectives and viewpoints. In Genesis 1-2 God reveals himself as the author of human life, and that culture is intrinsic to God's creation of humankind. These and other creation texts reveal that human differences are neither merely incidental nor surface-level. Instead, our differences are essential to us as human beings, and we should welcome and acknowledge them. Our differences in language, culture, kinship patterns, cultural conditioning, histories, and life experience guarantee that we will see, approach, and initially react to things in dramatically different ways.

> Acts 17.23-28 – "For as I passed along and observed the objects of your worship, I found also an altar with this inscription, 'To the unknown god.' What therefore you worship as unknown, this I proclaim to you. [24] The God who made the world and everything in it, being Lord of heaven and earth, does not live in temples made by man, [25] nor is he served by human hands, as though he needed anything, since he himself gives to all mankind life and breath and everything. [26] And he made from one man every nation of mankind to live on all the face of the earth, having determined allotted periods and the boundaries of their dwelling place, [27] that they should seek God, and perhaps feel their way toward him and find him. Yet he is actually not far from each one of us, [28] for 'In him we live and move and have our being'; as even some of your own poets have said, 'For we are indeed his offspring.'"

Truly, then, our God is the God of creation as well as covenant, the God of Gentiles as well as Jews (Rom. 3.28-30). Of course, our differences have been acknowledged and reconciled in Christ through his work on the cross (cf. Eph. 2.14-16 – For he himself is our peace, who has made us both one and has broken down in his flesh the dividing wall of hostility [15] by abolishing the law of commandments expressed in ordinances, that he might create in himself one new man in place of the two, so making peace). The goal of redemption now is to become Christlike (i.e., moral transformation), not to get other people to view things like we do in all matters (i.e., cultural sameness). Look at two key texts in the New Testament on the difference that difference plays in the Church:

> Gal. 3.27-28 – For as many of you as were baptized into Christ have put on Christ. [28] There is neither Jew nor Greek, there is neither slave nor free, there is no male and female, for you are all one in Christ Jesus.

> Col. 3.11 – Here there is not Greek and Jew, circumcised and uncircumcised, barbarian, Scythian, slave, free; but Christ is all, and in all.

Now that we know Christ, the goal is not that we merely or mindlessly conform to the same basic ideas about everything. Now, in Christ, all cultures are equally viable in the Christian worldview of peoples. Human culture is valid and affirmed, while the many human cultures are relative and vary.

The differences between people may not necessarily be bad or wrong. Every culture has elements that are amoral (disputes that arise from tastes, preferences, customs, traditions or habits). Some practices may even be moral (consistent with the way God desires us to act or think). And still, every culture will contain views and practices that are immoral (ways that contradict or are opposed to the way God desires us to be and do). These differences come out in our relationships and people express them in their discussions over ideas, actions, policies, values, and facts. Unfortunately, these differences tend to alienate and divide us, and if not settled with open, honest dialogue, may lead to prejudice, hatred, and even violence.

Good dialogue sees communication as a process, a circle of listening and responding, and engaging in conversation until clarity is won (cf. Appendix, *Toward a Hermeneutic of Critical Engagement*). Dialogue is helpful because through open discussion with others on contested issues we can become aware of our stereotypes, concepts, and viewpoints. We see how our various views may erect barriers, and cause us to treat people in ways that do not please God. Through dialogue, we can find new ways to relate to people with whom we disagree, and we can learn new, necessary skills and dispositions to help us connect to others who may think differently than we do. This kind of mature interaction is fundamental to living as Christ's disciple in a society where people hold dramatically different opinions about contested things, with as entirely diverse backgrounds and upbringing as we do.

Recognize that your verbal descriptions and the "facts of the matter" differ in certain fundamental respects. Our language maps can be helpful, but they have serious limitations in describing things as they were/are/will be.

"The Map Is Not the Territory."

To say that communication is a problem is to say nothing new, for men always have had to strive to make themselves understood. Each age, however, has its own peculiar communication problems; and our age, possessing as it does an amazing means for increasing, extending, and amplifying communication, confronts in the process both greater potential and greater frustration. While the mass media for communication have increased so that people today are bombarded with news and propaganda of all kinds, their understanding of and sensitivity to events and ideas seem to be decreasing.

~ Howe, *ibid.*, p. 18

To borrow language from semanticists and linguists, when dealing with a language we must realize that our verbal maps are not the same as the territory that we are describing. Words are words, and non-word realities are non-word realities. This notion is a simple idea. You can call a "chair" a "wallup" or a "shemback," but the thing you are sitting on (whatever you call it) will not change. Whatever word or term you call it, it is what it is. One of the first things you must learn about words is that they do not necessarily have to match the reality that they refer to; words can be abused easily!

If you drew a map with Chicago on the west coast of the US, and New York in the state of Florida, your map would be wrong. Anyone using your map would be in error, and worse, airliners or travelers following your map would wind up being completely confused and wrong. Can you imagine the waste of time and resources it would create if everyone in America used a map that said Chicago was where Los Angeles is? It would be disastrous, indeed!

A map, to be useful, has to reflect and match the territory, but it will never be a perfect reproduction of it. While you can draw a map that describes an area, the actual reality is much different. The best maps will be those that reflect the territory, that point to where Chicago is on its map, and not what the map maker prefers to indicate on his or her "personal" map. Maps that are useful are not merely "personal." We must remember that our viewpoints are like maps; they are useful only if our opinions square up with the facts and truth of the matter we are considering.

Perhaps you've heard the story of the "Six Blind Men and the Elephant" where six blind men touched differing parts of an elephant, and described it exclusively by the part they grabbed hold of. One held the trunk and declared the elephant to be like a "hose," another the ear, and declared it to be like a "fan." Another selected the tail and declared it to be like a "rope," and another the body of the elephant, stating it to be like a "wall." One touched the tusk, declaring elephants to be like a "spear," and the final man selected one of its legs stating that elephants are like a "tree trunk." In one sense, each blind person certainly possessed a piece of data (and were therefore correct in their "piece"), but none of them had the kind of verbal map that would prove sufficient to describe the whole elephant. We do the same when we fail to recognize that our limited, tiny maps may not fit the entire territory of the issue we are discussing. Good dialogue occurs when each person communicating realizes that their particular "slice" of truth may not be everything that can be said and understood on the question at hand.

This idea of mapping can also be explained in our ability to diagnose things carefully before you treat something. I have heard of the tragic cases where people went in to see their doctor for a relatively minor ailment, only to be misdiagnosed for some serious illness, and prescribed a treatment that was both unnecessary and unhelpful. Paul instructs the Thessalonicans to make the right diagnosis (or, to make the correct map of the territory) before they provide the appropriate response to

others, based on their evaluation of them. Look at his wise
advice on being careful in 1 Thessalonians 5.14 (see Appendix,
Discerning Root Issues):

> 1 Thess. 5.14 – And we urge you, brothers, admonish the
> idle, encourage the fainthearted, help the weak, be patient
> with them all.

You see Paul's insistence that the Thessalonians read the
situation right (give a correct diagnosis) before they applied
a proper response in their community. We could, too, go
back to our map idea; you have to draw a "map" based on
the actual "territory" before you go down any road of
encouragement or rebuke. You *admonish* the idle, not the
weak, and you *encourage* the fainthearted, not the idle!
You cannot appropriately engage a person without knowing
accurately where they are. Only then, can you provide the
kind of response that builds them up in their lives.

Connected to this principle of accurate verbal "map making,"
the footnote here provides a handful of helpful ideas that
semanticists use that can improve our ability to handle our
language in dialogue with greater clarity and helpfulness.[1]

---

1   For a fascinating and helpful understanding of dialogue, please read William
Isaacs, *Dialogue and the Art of Thinking Together*. New York: Doubleday Books,
1999; David Lochhead, *The Dialogical Imperative*. Maryknoll, NY: Orbis Press, 1988;
and Reuel Howe, *The Miracle of Dialogue*. Greenwich, Connecticut: Seabury Press,
1963. For understanding the role of language in communication, refer to Ken
Keyes, Jr., *Taming Your Mind*, St. Mary, KY: Living Love Publications, 1975.

PRINCIPLE 3
Non-allness. You simply can never know everything there is to know about anything, so show humility in expressing your opinions.

"So Far as I Know."

> A barrier to communication is something that keeps meanings from meeting. Meaning barriers exist between all people, making communication much more difficult than most people seem to realize. It is false to assume that if one can talk, he can communicate. Because so much of our education misleads people into thinking that communication is easier than it is, they become discouraged and give up when they run into difficulty. Because they do not understand the nature of the problem, they do not know what to do. The wonder is not that communication is as difficult as it is, but that it occurs as much as it does.
>
> ~ Howe, *ibid.*, pp. 23-24.

Once you realize that human beings differ in significant ways and that we all have different "maps" of the reality "territory," you then must also admit that no one can claim to know all there is to know about a person, place, or thing. Each person's knowledge of a particular issue or situation is limited to what they know, which may or may not be complete. Our thoughts and statements must be measured, and we should not pretend to speak with absolute full knowledge about anything we are discussing. We can and should use the phrase "So far as I know and understand, I believe that such and such is the case."

We should strive to keep an open mind for better arguments, more facts, and more thorough evidence, constantly remaining open to developing an "et cetera" mindset. The phrase *et cetera* literally means "and so forth"; it suggests that there is more to be known, said, and understood on a point, once it is made. A failure to admit that one cannot possibly know everything there is to say about anything results in a tendency to believe one's thoughts and judgment without revision. Christ asks us to judge not according to appearance but with "righteous judgment," the kind that is always open to the truth, wherever it may come from, or whoever may share it.

The Scriptures are highly critical of the person who pretends to know everything that they think they need to know. Paul exhorted the Corinthians, "Now concerning food offered to idols: we know that 'all of us possess knowledge.' This 'knowledge' puffs up, but love builds up. If anyone imagines that he knows something, *he does not yet know as he ought to know*. But if anyone loves God, he is known by God" (emphasis mine) (1 Cor. 8.1-3). Truly, it is only a matter of time before the person who is wise in his or her own conceit will suffer at the hands of their own pride and foolishness. "Do you see a man who is wise in his own eyes? There is more hope for a fool than for him" (Prov. 26.12).

Such people with this disposition place their lives in peril, and simply will never be open enough to honestly dialogue with others, to seek the truth in love. To speak the truth is a noteworthy goal. Speaking the truth involves speaking in light of all the facts (not just the ones which support your position!) and listening openly to the arguments and conclusions being drawn from those facts. In dialogue, we communicate to get at the heart of the matter in question and do so with respect and care. In these exchanges, we do not discuss matters to get brownie points or to show the other side that they are wrong. We readily admit when we are wrong, and have misjudged the facts or misinterpreted them. We listen to contrary ideas to see if they can help our clarity, and we do not aim to just "win" every exchange.

The apostle John says that our Lord was full of grace and truth (John 1.14). To speak the truth in love is to strive to be as Christ was with others; he was gracious, and he was truthful, as demonstrated in his many interactions with others. That these two great virtues can meet in dialogue is the goal of all good Christian communication – we simultaneously strive to tell the truth and to be loving and gracious to those with whom we engage. Inevitably, this will mean that we admit that we simply cannot and do not know everything there is to know about everything. Without this admission, a true dialogue will be impossible.

PRINCIPLE 4
We should qualify and "index" our judgments when referring to our knowledge of particular people, places, and things, and avoid stereotyping others.

"Which One of Those Are We Talking About?"

> Our anxieties cause us to make and to attempt to find affirmations of our own being, affirmations that may indeed threaten the being of others. Our need to be drives us to live lives of self-justification which can be a cause for uneasiness, if not enmity, in our fellows. Such ontological concern, with all the anxieties that cluster around it, makes it difficult to both speak and hear openly and honestly. This barrier to communication is built into human existence and stands between man and man in every instance. There are no exemptions.
>
> ~ Howe, *ibid.*, p. 25.

Because no two things are identical in all respects, we must be careful not to prejudge one person, idea, or situation to be identical to another person, idea, or situation. To do so is to stereotype another person or their arguments. Although stereotyping another is easy and convenient, it is not an accurate way to evaluate others and communicate with them. To stereotype is to simplify and standardize every individual member of a group with traits you believe all members of that group represent and share. This kind of dialogue is characterized by saying things like, "All Calvinists believe . . ." or "every woman knows . . ." and other overgeneralized statements. To say that all white people are X, or that all Baptists are Y, or that all people who baptize through sprinkling are wrong, is false and biased, on the surface. You will have to look at particular white people or specific Baptists or individual persons who baptize through sprinkling to make your point. You can't simply take a single person of a group, and paint them with all the traits you think are right about an entire group.

I am an African American middle-aged man. I am a "Black" man, and I cannot tell you how many times I have been treated a certain way or heard in a particular manner because my debate or dialogue partner knew things about "the Blacks." They judged me to be like all "Blacks" that they heard or read about, without looking at me at all.

Regardless of how I sought to help them know that Black life is not monolithic (i.e., that we all do not conspire to act and live in the same way everywhere) they clung to their notions of "Blacks,"often built on their own unique experiences with the "Blacks" in their own lives. If we are to dialogue with others, we need to put a check on our tendency to think that all people of a kind are alike, that all ideas that seem alike are alike, or that all situations which look similar must be identical. Black man1 is not Black man2.

This principle demands that you do not jump to conclusions, that you wait and hear a matter first before you pass judgment or make a statement. You cannot assume that you know people, things, or concepts *generally*; rather, when discussing a theme or issue, you seek to drill down on the *specific* facts before you pass judgment. The Bible insists on this approach, i.e., not jumping to conclusions about things generally, but making specific inquiry on what is the case *in this instance*:

> Prov. 18.13 – If one gives an answer before he hears, it is his folly and shame.

> John 7.24 – Do not judge by appearances, but judge with right judgment.

> John 7.50-51 – Nicodemus, who had gone to him before, and who was one of them, said to them, [51] "Does our law judge a man without first giving him a hearing and learning what he does?"

It is unwise to stereotype. To avoid this pitfall you must determine that you will be known not for your clever comebacks but from the depth of your ability to listen. You must let others speak – without interrupting, without putting words into their mouth, without being defensive of everything they say against you or your position, and without assuming anything in the dialogue. To let others speak means that you put the priority on actually listening to the other side. A dialogue is a listening session, first and foremost, before it is a discussion or debate session. The more you can concentrate on developing your skills as a listener, the less you will be prone to view everything in black-and-white terms.

In the end, your response to the words and arguments of those you disagree with may wind up persuading others to your viewpoint rather than you shouting your view over theirs. Make it your first priority to listen to what others say, and to know that things aren't usually given to us in neat this-or-that categories. Above all else, commit to listening well in every exchange with others. If you make this approach the heart and soul of your dialogical approach, you will not only communicate better, you will also become a better person. Through this, you will learn patience, to wait your turn before you speak, and to understand the other side before you criticize it. You will suspend your judgment until you hear the evidence, and you will report what they believe back to them with respect and clarity. This kind of dialogue will help you discover the truth, and make you a more productive, more open human being as well.

Things may act and appear very different, depending on where you are when you describe it, and the place you view it.

"From Where I Stand."

> The principle underlying dialogue is: "He who loses his life for my sake and the Gospel shall find it." This means that we enter into relationship not for the purpose of gaining, but for the purpose of giving, with the prayer that we may lose our pretentions, our defensive need to justify ourselves, and gain, instead, a reassurance of life by having it affirmed in our relationship with another.
>
> The importance of courage in dialogue deserves extended consideration. And while the specific instance of it we are discussing is taken from teaching, all that we are saying about it is equally applicable to every situation in which dialogue is possible.
>
> ~ Howe, *ibid.*, p. 97.

This principle affirms the simple truth that things appear differently to people depending on what they bring to the dialogue. While all of us want to think that we are objective, clear, and unbiased about everything that we discuss, debate, or communicate, if we were honest, the opposite is the case. Our views depend on all kinds of things that are unique to our experience – our heredity, training, interests, and life journey. All of our lived experience helps us to form a single and personal "vantage point," a place where we stand to evaluate the question under consideration. No one can see over fences or around corners: you can only see (and therefore dialogue about) the things you know and understand from the spot and position you are currently standing on.

Of course, this is not negative, to assert that we are human. We have lived out our lives and "we know what we know"; we see and understand things through our own unique (and historically conditioned) vantage point. However, our personal view is oftentimes not the only viable position or possible conclusion on a question. "The one who states his case first seems right, until the other comes and examines him" (Prov. 18.17). We should state our case and admit our view, which is based on our understanding of the facts and the question. Your view has been shaped by your experience (i.e., where you have been and by where you are standing). It may or may not be true! Outside of the Lord himself, no human being can see or understand things from "all points of view." Our opinions are built on our understandings, and things will appear differently to us because of where we are and how we have lived. Every person everywhere must admit this; to fail to acknowledge this is to continually claim that your angle of vision is the only legitimate angle worth considering! We are prone to use our own judgments and story to determine the truthfulness of all judgments and all stories (see Appendix, *The Cycle of Selfish Preoccupation*). You can literally keep your life if you will keep your habits of seeing the world "through your eyes only" under control. "Whoever restrains his words has knowledge, and he who has a cool spirit is a man of understanding. Even a fool who keeps silent is considered wise; when he closes his lips, he is deemed intelligent" (Prov. 17.27-28).

Let's be honest. People can look at the same facts, consider the same situation, and come to opposite understandings of what those facts and circumstances mean, and how we ought to interpret them. You can assert your values, ideas, and opinions as your own; they are yours, and you claim them. Yet, you cannot consider, as a matter of course, that your values are the only ones that exist or the only ones that should exist. This is precisely why dialogue, discussion, and debate is necessary.

Can you present your ideas and argument with clear logic and valid evidence in such a way that people who, at the beginning of the conversation felt entirely different than you, change their opinion after hearing you? This movement from skepticism to commitment is the purpose of dialogue and represents the trophy of open and honest communication. You cannot claim the prize if you refuse to play the game! Admit that you have a view, and embrace your responsibility in dialogue to help others see that yours is the "truer" perspective.

PRINCIPLE 6
Varying degrees. Things exist and come to be in varying degrees, on a scale from nothing to everything, and rarely on an all-or-none basis.

"Up to a Point."

> The same word, for instance, can have different meaning for different persons even though long usage has made standard its meaning. Allowance must always be made, however, for wide ranges of nuances and variations born of individual associations and experiences. The word "father," for example, has standard meaning, but each person brings to it his own special meanings which may vary so much that its use is no guarantee of communication. A word means what the speaker intends it to mean, but the personal equivalences for the bearer may differ.
>
> ~ Howe, *ibid.*, p. 29.

When in discussion with people on various facts, topics, and ideas, things are usually not merely black or white, up or down, all bad or all good. Most views and opinions contain a range of things, somewhere between zero to a hundred, and don't allow for us to call them "all haters" while we are "fully loving." Such kinds of either-or habits of thinking often tend to sabotage open dialogue and makes you unable to see any good, truth, beauty, or right in any position other than your own.

If we were honest, we would agree with the bold claim in Jeremiah: "The heart is deceitful above all things, and desperately sick; who can understand it? I the LORD search the heart and test the mind, to give every man according to his ways, according to the fruit of his deeds" (Jer. 17.9-10). The claim here is that our vantage point is limited, skewed, deceitful. No one can claim complete objectivity. We should enter into all discussion and dialogue with humility and openness, ready and willing to learn from others, and to learn about ourselves.

Dialogue and debate demand an honest admission that each person's view may have both negative and positive attributes. Either-or thinking tends to be misleading, unhelpful, extreme, and contrary to open sharing of various opinions on a problematic theme or subject. As a dialogue partner, you must refrain from characterizing the other side as "the Evil Empire," while referring to you and your colleagues as "the righteous Jedi warriors." To be trapped in either-or thinking is to welcome all kinds of unhelpful habits which make it nearly impossible for you to see any motive or substance of good in a position contrary to your own.

Are all Republicans greedy capitalists and all Democrats immoral liberals? Should you believe that baptism by immersion is "the only legitimate way to baptize," or that "no woman is given the gift of teaching by the Holy Spirit"? Do you think that "all foreigners are untrustworthy," or do you think that "you either work for a living or you're a lazy bum"? This kind of thinking refuses to survey the territory to see what truly is the case. Are people purely good or purely evil? Must a course of action be either perfectly divine or certainly demonic? Must we always view every conversation as a "somebody has to win" and "somebody has to lose" proposition? Can we both "win"? If neither of us is right, shouldn't we both "lose"?

This principle admits that often there can be more than one good answer or solution to any particular problem or issue. You must allow for dialogue to work, in other words, to see if through dialogue viable alternative positions emerge and can be defended. The goal of open communication is not to get the other side to surrender to the brilliance of our logic and argument, or to get them to admit that they are wrong and we are right. Preferably, the goal of open and mature dialogue is to seek mutual understanding on a particular matter, even if its means that we "agree to disagree" on the subject under discussion. Dialogue's goal is never to make our dialogue partner submit to us, or surrender to our viewpoint, or to yield their convictions to us without being persuaded by our logic and evidence.

Young, inexperienced dialogue partners possess only a single vision of what dialogue and discussion must become. In their view, argument is war. The idea that argument is war is an old and established principle in our society. We talk about taking people's points down, or holding our position against another's attack, or making headway or gaining new ground in advancing a particular claim or idea. The problem with thinking about argument and dialogue only in this way is that it makes you susceptible to see every dialogue as a fight, a skirmish, a cage battle. While it is vital to discuss tough issues passionately, we engage in dialogue to understand different opinions and sides of an issue and seek to persuade another that our views provide better, truer, and more accurate views of what is desirable and what is true. Debate is a living principle in our Western societies, especially in venues of law, Congress, academic discussion, science and politics. So all of us must learn to share our views, knowing that others hold their opinions in opposite ways to ours, and just as sincerely as we do.

Godly, sincere, and biblical folk should be able to discuss controversial and difficult issues without always resorting to games of war, setting up communication defenses, or engaging in plain old-fashioned rudeness. The goal of dialogue is mutual understanding, the kind that leads to good decisions and wise practices. This won't always result in a full agreement, though. Sometimes dialogue will lead sincere folk to express their differences openly. Other times, dialogue will lead both partners to modify their views, informed by the other's case and claims. Whether it ends in agreement or just mutual recognition of our varying views, we should embrace the kind of exchanges that help us to listen well, speak truthfully, and move our communication forward. Above all else, dialogue must be grounded on mutual respect: for our own opinions, our dialogue partners, and for the truth.

A dialogue will prove to be a failure if you cannot affirm that things rarely exist in all-or-nothing kind of categories. Frankly stated, we grow in our understandings and appreciations of what is true, beautiful, and good. We need to admit this in all dialogue, and deliberately look (and look hard!) for the truth and the right in our opposition's position. Don't start your conversations with a "they're wrong, we're right" mode. Listen to the arguments, the evidence, and the ideas, and test everything that comes before you. Hold fast to what is true, and let go of what is untrue.

Also, admit it quickly when your dialogue partner tells the truth, and don't hide from the fact that the conversation may expose the weakness and illogical nature of your own position. Simply put: tell the truth, letting God be true and every man a liar. Jesus is the truth, speaks the truth, and everyone who declares the truth hears his voice. You don't own it, and we all have to search for it. Don't claim before the dialogue begins that you and you alone are privy to the truth, that only you see the facts, and that your position alone concurs with what is best. Listen, and judge with righteous judgment.

Give clear, unbiased receipt to the opinions and viewpoints that have been voiced in the dialogue.

"This is what *I* hear you saying – is that right?"

> Teachers and ministers seem to suffer widely from what I call "agenda anxiety," the anxiety to get across all the points of whatever subject they are dealing with, regardless of the state of being of those whom they are teaching. For them communication means covering the subject matter to their satisfaction. Unfortunately, one can be satisfied with his coverage of content and still fail to communicate. People have been heard to exclaim after a lecture, "Wasn't that wonderful!" But when they were asked what the lecturer said, they had to admit that they did not remember. The destructive element in agenda anxiety is that we are more concerned about data and its comprehensive coverage than we are about truth.
>
> ~ Howe, *ibid.*, p. 30.

To listen well, not anxiously so you can make your point or put the other side down, demands that you act like a mirror. The funny thing about a mirror is that it offers no judgment about what it reflects; it merely indicates back what stands before it. All dialogue that is good dialogue captures this kind of mirroring activity, i.e., the ability to give a clear, unbiased, and untainted paraphrase of what a person is saying. In dialogue we let each person say what they mean, and interpret their own language. When we are deeply engaged in hot or fierce debate, it is easy to "lie" about your opponents view, to ascribe things to them that they did not say and do not believe, and to twist what they said to mean things that they never intended.

There is a tendency in all hotly contested discussions to interrupt the other person. They state a couple of words, and we believe that we instantly know what they are about to say, that it is wrong, and that you can crush it before it is even said! In the fray of discussions, we don't listen, we are not careful, we jump to conclusions, and we point fingers. This principle encourages you to be quiet long enough to hear what the other is saying, make sure you know what it means, and repeat it back to them, to get their agreement that your understanding is what they mean to say. This demands self-control; not *will* power (power to interrupt) but *won't* power (power to be silent until you know what the other is saying, and what they mean). "Whoever trusts in his own mind is a fool, but he who walks in wisdom will be delivered" (Prov. 28.26).

Rather than false, bigoted tactics, good dialogue partners give a clean receipt to another person's opinion or views. In other words, they seek to give back to their dialogue partner their own words with the meanings and interpretations that they offered when they gave them. Like the mirror, we want to represent clearly and objectively what our conversational partners mean by what they are saying, in their own words and images.

It goes without saying that the most important thing that a person can do in this kind of conversation is to learn how to listen well.

> Prov. 8.32-35 – And now, O sons, listen to me: blessed are those who keep my ways. [33] Hear instruction and be wise, and do not neglect it. [34] Blessed is the one who listens to me, watching daily at my gates, waiting beside my doors. [35] For whoever finds me finds life and obtains favor from the LORD.

> Eccles. 5.1-3 – Guard your steps when you go to the house of God. To draw near to listen is better than to offer the sacrifice of fools, for they do not know that they are doing evil. [2] Be not rash with your mouth, nor let your heart be hasty to utter a word before God, for God is in heaven and you are on earth. Therefore let your words be few. [3] For a dream comes with much business, and a fool's voice with many words.

> Prov. 10.19 – When words are many, transgression is not lacking, but whoever restrains his lips is prudent.

> Prov. 13.3 – Whoever guards his mouth preserves his life; he who opens wide his lips comes to ruin.

> Prov. 15.2 – The tongue of the wise commends knowledge, but the mouths of fools pour out folly.

Listening is not an easy task, but you can master it if you are willing to learn a few basic principles about the nature of good communication. Whenever you discuss anything with anyone, it is important that you refuse to make them appear to say things that they never intended to say. In other words, make sure that you hear what they say, and paraphrase their argument honestly and openly in your reply. This is neither easy nor fun, especially in the midst of hotly contested communication. Do not take an open, polite, and considerate approach for granted. You must strive to hear what they are saying, clarify when it is not clear, and paraphrase what you think they are saying after they have said it. Let them correct your hearing, if it is wrong, and allow them to do so without interruption or twisting their meaning. The simplest way to ensure that you heard a person say what you thought they said is to give their words and meanings back to them, in your own words.

This principle is formative for good dialogue, for several reasons. First, many problems occur because we easily mishear others, thinking they said something they never said. You cannot assume that you understand what a person means by the words they use. Take the time to listen carefully without judging or prejudice, and then paraphrase in your own words what you think you just heard them say. Give them the option to clear up your rendering, to correct it, if necessary. This process ensures that you will know what they mean by the words they use. What is important is not that you give your clever answers back; instead, dialogue is built on a search for understanding, and begins when you carefully and fairly rephrase their argument in a way that they say reflects what they mean.

To do this well demands patience – patience to listen, and carefully paraphrase what they are saying and mean. The critical skill to apply here is the art of being charitable and fair in all discussions with everyone about anything. You must learn to answer others in a fair and open manner, not to twist or to misread what they say only to pour your meanings into what they spoke. To answer reasonably means that you let them say what they want, and mean what they want. The worst thing you can do with a dialogue partner is to wrongly suggest meanings to their words that you know they did not intend to mean. This tactic is both false and unfair and will prove irritating to your dialogue partner. Ultimately, this lying practice will undermine your communication and relationship with the other person.

PRINCIPLE 8
Answer fully every dialogue partner's question concerning your own language and its meaning.

"Is there anything I can clarify to help you understand my viewpoint?"

> Dialogue is that address and response between persons in which there is a flow of meaning between them in spite of all the obstacles that normally would block the relationship. It is that interaction between persons in which one of them seeks to give himself as he is to the other, and also seeks to know the other as the other is. This means that he will not attempt to impose his truth and view on the other. Such is the relationship which characterizes dialogue and is the precondition to dialogical communication.
>
> ~ Howe, *ibid.*, p. 37.

Once you have given receipt to what someone has said, and you've committed yourself to answering your dialogue partner in a fair and open way, it will be important to answer them fully. One tactic of unclear communication is to ignore your dialogue partner's questions about what you mean when you use certain language or terms. This refusal to be clear is bold hypocrisy. This is an underhanded way of avoiding real communication. You owe your dialogue partner the level of openness that will address any and all questions they have about your use of language, and what you mean when you use your language.

For example, if you offered your dialogue partner three reasons for why you think they should believe that such and such is the case, don't shy away from explaining those reasons carefully to them. The burden is on you to be clear, for the "burden of proof" is on the person making a claim. If you contend for your claim, for your point, to convince others to hold your views, you must be fair. This means that you must answer open and honest questions composed about a conviction, as it is not fair to only answer one of the things that they just shared. Open communication will demand that you listen to all three points, listen to the evidence and arguments given for all three points, and then respond in turn to each one of the three points. This is the meaning of "answering fully," the idea of giving an open and clear response to what you heard.

Nothing is more frustrating in dialogue than to be in a discussion where the other side is deliberately twisting your meanings. To reverse the order of presentation, if your dialogue partner offers you three reasons for some point, or provides three aspects of a particular plan, or suggests three benefits of a particular action, listen to the entire argument. Give receipt to all three points, and answer each one. You take them seriously when you thoroughly answer them, engaging all their rebuttals and claims, and not omitting a single one in your reply. To leave things out is a form of rhetorical gamesmanship, and undermines open communication.

This principle highlights how important it is to be gracious in our words, approaches, and dialogue processes. Answering your dialogue partner's questions mean that you are seeking to be gracious – you are fair, generous, and open to their questions. In other words, you want to clarify your position, not to get a "gotcha" moment in, but that they can know what you believe, and why. To be gracious means that we have to be generous in the conversation, giving them time and room to share their views. We need to learn how to think the best about the other side, allowing them to have their own opinions and conclusions from their read of the evidence. Good dialogue affirms the other side's right to differ with us and will avoid any efforts to shame or disrespect them as they share their ideas. This takes much discipline, time, and prayer, but you can become the kind of person whose words are gracious, whose opinions about the other side are not false or prejudiced. "Whoever keeps his mouth and his tongue keeps himself out of trouble" (Prov. 21.23).

This does not mean, of course, that we mindlessly agree with everything that our dialogue partner says, expresses, or argues. No. We hold our positions with integrity, based on our thinking and read of the evidence. We should stand ready to engage others with why we hold our positions, wherever we can. What it does mean, however, is that we never disrespect others in dialogue, but speak the truth graciously, openly, and honestly, for the sake of understanding and truth. Being gracious in dialogue is not the same as being flaky or gullible. It is, however, to be open-minded, to never interrupt or falsify their opinions, to listen first, and give receipt to what they believe. We do not automatically surrender our positions in dialogue or give up our dearly held commitments to the truth. We do share our dearly held convictions with fairness and an open heart to God and to them. We begin and end with respect and love, for them and the truth.

PRINCIPLE 9
Refuse every inclination and temptation to treat the other side with disrespect, or to be dismissive or rude in your exchanges.

"Let's start again, for this is important for us to think through, together."

"Experiencing the other side" is Buber's phrase for identifying the nature of dialogue, and by it he means to feel an event from the side of the person one meets as well as from one's own side. And so the true teacher accepts, as a part of the discipline of his profession, the responsibility to "be aware of the meaning of a course from the student's point of View and to be alert to the meaning of his side of the learning situation. Education, relationships, love, and communication that are not dialogical, are evil because they exploit and seek to appropriate. Much education and communication, to say nothing of love and relationship, are evil and destructive. The same can be said for much religion when it emphasizes an attitude that turns one in on oneself.

~ Howe, *ibid.*, pp. 38-39.

This relates to the previous idea, and yet deserves its careful place. Simply put, a key element in healthy dialogical exchange and godly debate is a refusal to be rude. The Scriptures are clear that love is not rude. If your position is true, and your evidence is solid, and your arguments are clear, then you should not have to speak or shout over, poke fun at, or seek to shame others or caricature them or their beliefs. Many rhetorical blunders are rooted in aiming your comments at the person and not at the point. If your ideas and arguments are persuasive, you do not have to be rude, hateful, or irritating to your dialogue partner. Those who continuously denigrate their dialogue partner's motives, intentions and abilities prove the weakness of their character and argument. If you are right, then you should be able to defend your view without sharing rude, unclear and unhelpful comments aimed at the other side.

This skill is difficult for those who are new to effective communication and good dialogue. It is all too easy to get trapped in a mindset that those who hold bad opinions are essentially bad people. This idea represents a fundamental error in communication. A person can be wrong in their thinking and still be worthwhile in their person. The cancer of ungodly dialogue is the rude, shameful exchanges aimed at humiliating people and not to clarify positions. Crude people use a free and open exchange to share words with malicious intent, designed to hurt and shame others. Such talking is not dialogue at all. You must strive always to take and keep the high ground of open-minded and fair discussion. Doing this will change the atmosphere of your communication. Not only will you be able to get to the truth quicker, without hard feelings or bitter attitudes, but you come to respect and honor those on the other side, even if you do not agree with their view.

The simplest way to avoid rudeness in dialogue is to suspend judgment until you have actually heard and understood the other side. Allowing others to express their viewpoint openly is a gift, a gift of love and mutual respect. This demands that you allow them time to share their views and their evidence. You must suspend your judgment until they present their side. You should not engage until you know what they believe. Suspension of judgment, linked with an open listening heart, will ensure that you understand their view before you criticize, and hear rightly their opinion before you weigh its value.

As mentioned before, you need not pretend to have no view on the matter. Of course, you do! Furthermore, you believe your opinion is the correct view. In every serious discussion those communicating are convinced of their own views and read of the issues and the evidence. This is normal and good. I do not here advocate that you pretend to have no viewpoint; what I am suggesting, however, is that you listen to the other side's claims before you engage them. Dialogue does not mean that you do not have a rebuttal against their side; it does mean, though, that you refuse to answer before you understand what their case is, and why they believe it to be so.

Cases made in a court of law, formal debates of the US Senate, and open forums on tough issues all offer a clear picture of what it means to respectfully and yet critically discuss arguments. These kinds of exchanges lead to better decisions, ideas, and policies. These venues demand that we refuse to turn truth-seeking activities into name-calling. Don't be discouraged if it takes some time to perfect this dialogical skill. It takes internal discipline to listen to the other side without shaming, ignoring, or misrepresenting it. When you do, actual dialogue can occur.

PRINCIPLE 10
Dialogue is a process, not a destination.
Learn that everyone and everything changes
in significant ways, over time.

"As of Today, I Believe This Is the Case . . . But I Am Open to Dialogue."

Dialogue has more respect for a responsible No and all that it signifies than for an irresponsible Yes. Because monologue seeks always to speak the concluding word, a negative response is seen to have no future and must therefore stand as a sign of failure in communication. The word of dialogue, on the other hand, since it is a beginning word, is able to accept the negative response as part of the dialogue, and instead of regarding it as a sign of failure sees it as a part of the process in which a person moves from one point of view or conviction to another. It is necessary for us some times to say No before we can say Yes.

~ Howe, ibid, p. 58.

Our final principle suggests that no one should see dialogue as a temporary fix or an easy solution to resolve difficult and tough issues. Dialogue asserts that everything and everyone is changing, that those changes are taking place in significant ways that affect everything around us, and that, over time, our views and experiences will shift. The better we become at dialogue with others, the more we will see that dialogue must become a way of life, a set course for us if we intend to arrive at mutual understanding, better decisions, and ultimately, to a better comprehension of what is true and best. Our ever-changing world demands that we make dialogue a way of life, a disposition, and a manner of our living in the world and relating to others.

Here's the truth: everything and everyone is changing, and both can either grow or contract, based on their reactions. I personally can attest that I have changed much in my attitudes, behaviors, and viewpoints, over time. I grew up in the 1960s, a season of free love, rock music, societal upheaval, and national discord over the war in Vietnam. I can barely understand (or even tolerate!) the young black boy I used to be, the one who got mixed up in the free-love drug culture on a journey to discover the meaning of life! To be candid, I do not count myself to be that same young man of the 60s. I have changed dramatically over the last decades, and my viewpoints and ideas about nearly everything have changed.

Moreover, I no longer embrace the same philosophies or viewpoints about the "big ideas and questions of life" that I used to believe and argue for, and defend. I have been transformed in my views of sex, government, power, wealth, music, art, religion, and the afterlife. Don Davis (1969) is simply not the same person as Don Davis (2018)! You understand dialogue when you realize that people can change through it. Every person exists on a point on their life journey line somewhere between birth and death. It is both unfair and wrong to suggest that no one can change, or that we are

enslaved to see life as we have always seen it. This kind
of thought gives rise to using labels, code words, and false
judgments about others that deny their ability to grow.
My conclusions as a young man (Don Davis [1969]) were
dramatically opposite of my views today (Don Davis [2018]).
We are all changing, growing, learning, adapting. Thank God,
we can all come to see things more honestly as we learn to
engage in respectful dialogue with others.

Although this final principle is a simple idea, one that everyone
should acknowledge and embrace, you would be surprised to
learn that many dialogues occur without its application. People
can grow through dialogue with others. Communication is
not your opportunity and license to ram your opinions down
some unwilling person's throat! Rather, dialogue is about
open and honest engagement with another person who is
in process of forming their viewpoints, perspectives, and
commitments, even as you are. Such soul-building work
demands careful listening, thinking, and fair and open
interpretation of another's views. It also requires a deter-
mination above all else to be clear – to be willing to admit
when we are wrong, direct when we do not agree, and
always open to having our convictions and judgments
weighed by the evidence, argument, and rebuttal of the
"other side."

In other words, there can be no dialogue without integrity,
without character – the people engaged in the conversation
must be honest, clear, open, and willing to yield to the truth.
Dialogue is not about winning fights, but a legitimate search
for truth, even if that means we discover that we cannot
come to the same viewpoint on a particular matter. Even then,
we may elect to "keep the conversation going," to strive yet

more to see the other side. Dialogue dies when either side is unwilling to engage another in a search for truth. Understanding, not agreement, is the goal of all true dialogue.

So, learn to be quiet as you listen to others, and share your responses calmly, slowly, and confidently. Wait till you understand what the other person is saying, and don't comment until you do. These kinds of habits require deference, maturity, and insight to know when to speak and when not to. I believe that gaining knowledge is a slow process through shared communication, mutual respect, and diligent searching. I view knowledge as a journey, where the seekers move from a place of ignorance to a place of illumination to a place of testimony and witness (see Appendix, *From Deep Ignorance to Credible Witness*). We must give ourselves and others the time to learn, and not believe that truth can be mastered quickly, like throwing on a light switch. We must learn together, over time, with respect. As a rule of thumb, we should always inquire first, clarify statements, and then respond. Do not speak before you understand what you're going to say. Do not judge until you are sure you know what the other has said. Put a high premium on listening, on clarifying and asking questions, and making sure you know what the other person is saying. As you do, so your character and understanding will also grow.

Cultivating these habits can transform habits of engaging in loud argument into clear conversations of edifying dialogue. Remember Paul's injunction in Ephesians 4.14-15: speak the truth and speak it in love. We do not speak to win arguments, to shame the misguided, to defeat the ignorant, or browbeat our enemies! No. Instead, we speak to win people, to help them understand things in such a way that it will lead to their conversion, transformation, and edification. We are not here to win contests, but rather are here to touch hearts with the truth in Christ.

Several appendices speak directly to the power of learning to apply these principles faithfully and diligently. *The Hump* speaks of the challenges that any activity, like learning how to engage in godly dialogue, poses for the person just starting. The difficulty of learning these principles is immediately evident to the novice, the person who is accustomed only to sharing their own ideas, without regard for what others think. Only with the diligent, ongoing commitment to *gain skill* at dialogical conversation can a person overwhelm the resistance and inertia generated from simply "saying what's on my mind." To go from the untutored, out-of-control communication that many of us have to a careful, thoughtful open dialogue that is both respectful and truth seeking demands effort. No one learns this important skill quickly or easily. The results of disciplined application, however, prove to be more than we could possibly imagine.

Finally, two additional appendices highlight the need for constant, determined practice: *The Importance of Discipline* and *The Way of Wisdom*. Disciplined practice of the right principles produces the kind of skill and maturity we need to engage others with respect and clarity, and the way of wisdom (from a biblical viewpoint) requires a process of constant application and correction. To put it simply, no one can become truly skilled in dialogue without both understanding and applying the principles outlined in this little text, and apply it with enough perseverance as to ensure that new habits of communication are formed, and new kinds of conversation are engaged in.

Dear friend and fellow dialogue partner, we *can* learn, but we cannot quit. We have to engage, and we have to continue until we gain skill at dialogue. When we do, the Spirit can use us in multiple situations to bring light where there is shadow, truth where there is falsehood, and understanding where there is hatred. All we need do is to never give up (Appendix, *Boiling Down to the One*). We must desire, above all else, commitment to the truth. You must seek the truth, the truth that sets free, that believes that Christ is Lord, his Kingdom is real, and his Church is his agent and people. All other centers of thought and authority must yield to his truth: Jesus Christ is Lord, the center of all things, and every other issue and thing must be considered in his light (Appendix, *Substitute Centers*).

Dialogue is a journey, and as such, requires your steady, daily, and ongoing attention. You can learn this, if you yield to Christ, and seek truth from the heart. Let his word be the final word on this matter: "So Jesus said to the Jews who had believed him, 'If you abide in my word, you are truly my disciples, and you will know the truth, and the truth will set you free'" (John 8.31-32). Abide in his word, seek the truth in your dialogue, and prove the Savior right: the truth will set you free.

Epilogue

We have come to an end of our discussion of the nature of dialogue, but your journey into its richness has only just begun. I pray that your meditation on these truths will make you wise and clear in your communication. May the Lord be gracious to you in all the situations where you dialogue with others – in your marriage and family, with your friends and associates, and yes, even with those with whom you disagree. God will grant you the strength to be filled with his grace and truth, as our Lord was, Jesus of Nazareth, who spoke so graciously with others so long ago. He can still speak through us today if we allow him the freedom to do so.

Appendix

A Listing of Key Biblical Texts on the Tongue and Power of Words

Don L. Davis

Here is a handy list of some of the major texts of the Scriptures on the use of the tongue. The Bible has much to say on the impact of words on our lives, and contrasts in many places "the tongue of the wise" with the "mouth of the fool." The principles of dialogue mentioned in this text have been informed from this body of biblical literature. The entire body of the Scriptures below have been taken from the English Standard Version, for your use and reference.

The tongue possesses the power of life and death

Prov. 18.21 – Death and life are in the power of the tongue, and those who love it will eat its fruits.

James 3.1-12 – Not many of you should become teachers, my brothers, for you know that we who teach will be judged with greater strictness. [2] For we all stumble in many ways. And if anyone does not stumble in what he says, he is a perfect man, able also to bridle his whole body. [3] If we put bits into the mouths of horses so that they obey us, we guide their whole bodies as well. [4] Look at the ships also: though they are so large and are driven by strong winds, they are guided by a very small rudder wherever the will of the pilot directs. [5] So also the tongue is a small member, yet it boasts of great things. How great a forest is set ablaze by such a small fire! [6] And the tongue is a fire, a world of unrighteousness. The tongue is set among our members, staining the whole body, setting on fire the entire course of life, and set on fire by hell. [7] For every kind of beast and bird, of reptile and sea creature, can be tamed and has been tamed by mankind, [8] but no human being can tame the tongue. It is a restless evil, full of deadly poison. [9] With it we bless our Lord and Father, and with it we curse people who are made in the likeness of God. [10] From the same mouth come blessing and cursing. My brothers, these things ought not to be so. [11] Does a spring pour forth from the same opening both fresh and salt water? [12] Can a fig tree, my brothers, bear olives, or a grapevine produce figs? Neither can a salt pond yield fresh water.

Prov. 15.2 – The tongue of the wise commends knowledge, but the mouths of fools pour out folly.

Prov. 15.4 – A gentle tongue is a tree of life, but perverseness in it breaks the spirit.

Your communication can either uplift or devastate and harm

Prov. 12.13-14 – An evil man is ensnared by the transgression of his lips, but the righteous escapes from trouble. [14] From the fruit of his mouth a man is satisfied with good, and the work of a man's hand comes back to him.

Ps. 140.9 – As for the head of those who surround me, let the mischief of their lips overwhelm them!

Prov. 10.14 – The wise lay up knowledge, but the mouth of a fool brings ruin near.

Prov. 13.3 – Whoever guards his mouth preserves his life; he who opens wide his lips comes to ruin.

Prov. 14.3 – By the mouth of a fool comes a rod for his back, but the lips of the wise will preserve them.

Prov. 18.6-7 – A fool's lips walk into a fight, and his mouth invites a beating. [7] A fool's mouth is his ruin, and his lips are a snare to his soul.

Prov. 18.20 – From the fruit of a man's mouth his stomach is satisfied; he is satisfied by the yield of his lips.

Prov. 21.23 – Whoever keeps his mouth and his tongue keeps himself out of trouble.

Eccles. 10.12-14 – The words of a wise man's mouth win him favor, but the lips of a fool consume him. [13] The beginning of the words of his mouth is foolishness, and the end of his talk is evil madness. [14] A fool multiplies words, though no man knows what is to be, and who can tell him what will be after him?

The use of language and words reveal the depth of one's character, whether godly or unholy

Matt. 12.34-37 – You brood of vipers! How can you speak good, when you are evil? For out of the abundance of the heart the mouth speaks. [35] The good person out of his good treasure brings forth good, and the evil person out of his evil treasure brings forth evil. [36] I tell you, on the day of judgment people will give account for every careless word they speak, [37] for by your words you will be justified, and by your words you will be condemned."

Ps. 5.9 – For there is no truth in their mouth; their inmost self is destruction; their throat is an open grave; they flatter with their tongue.

Ps. 15.1-5 – O LORD, who shall sojourn in your tent? Who shall dwell on your holy hill? [2] He who walks blamelessly and does what is right and speaks truth in his heart; [3] who does not slander with his tongue and does no evil to his neighbor, nor takes up a reproach against his friend; [4] in whose eyes a vile person is despised, but who honors those who fear the LORD; who swears to his own hurt and does not change; [5] who does not put out his money at interest and does not take a bribe against the innocent. He who does these things shall never be moved.

Matt. 15.10-20 – And he called the people to him and said to them, "Hear and understand: [11] it is not what goes into the mouth that defiles a person, but what comes out of the mouth; this defiles a person." [12] Then the disciples came and said to him, "Do you know that the Pharisees were offended when they heard this saying?" [13] He answered, "Every plant that my heavenly Father has not planted will be rooted up. [14] Let them alone; they are blind guides. And if the blind lead the blind, both will fall into a pit." [15] But Peter said to him, "Explain the parable to us." [16] And he said, "Are you also still without understanding? [17] Do you not see that whatever goes into the mouth passes into the stomach and is expelled? [18] But what comes out of the mouth proceeds from the heart, and this defiles a person. [19] For out of the heart come evil thoughts, murder, adultery, sexual immorality, theft, false witness, slander. [20] These are what defile a person. But to eat with unwashed hands does not defile anyone."

Mark 7.14-15 – And he called the people to him again and said to them, "Hear me, all of you, and understand: [15] There is nothing outside a person that by going into him can defile him, but the things that come out of a person are what defile him."

Mark 7.17-23 – And when he had entered the house and left the people, his disciples asked him about the parable. [18] And he said to them, "Then are you also without understanding? Do you not see that whatever goes into a person from outside cannot defile him, [19] since it enters not his heart but his stomach, and is expelled?" (Thus he declared all foods clean.) [20] And he said, "What comes out of a person is what defiles him. [21] For from within, out of the heart of man, come evil thoughts, sexual immorality, theft, murder, adultery, [22] coveting, wickedness, deceit, sensuality, envy, slander, pride, foolishness. [23] All these evil things come from within, and they defile a person."

Luke 6.45 – The good person out of the good treasure of his heart produces good, and the evil person out of his evil treasure produces evil, for out of the abundance of the heart his mouth speaks.

James 1.26 – If anyone thinks he is religious and does not bridle his tongue but deceives his heart, this person's religion is worthless.

Rev. 14.5 – and in their mouth no lie was found, for they are blameless.

False, deceptive words produce lasting and harmful effects

Prov. 11.9 – With his mouth the godless man would destroy his neighbor, but by knowledge the righteous are delivered.

Job 19.2 – How long will you torment me and break me in pieces with words?

Ps. 55.20-21 – My companion stretched out his hand against his friends; he violated his covenant. [21] His speech was smooth as butter, yet war was in his heart; his words were softer than oil, yet they were drawn swords.

Ps. 57.4 – My soul is in the midst of lions; I lie down amid fiery beasts— the children of man, whose teeth are spears and arrows, whose tongues are sharp swords.

Ps. 64.3-4 – who whet their tongues like swords, who aim bitter words like arrows, [4] shooting from ambush at the blameless, shooting at him suddenly and without fear.

Ps. 140.3 – They make their tongue sharp as a serpent's, and under their lips is the venom of asps. Selah

Prov. 11.11 – By the blessing of the upright a city is exalted, but by the mouth of the wicked it is overthrown.

Prov. 12.6 – The words of the wicked lie in wait for blood, but the mouth of the upright delivers them.

Prov. 12.18 – There is one whose rash words are like sword thrusts, but the tongue of the wise brings healing.

Prov. 16.27 – A worthless man plots evil, and his speech is like a scorching fire. Words rightly spoken can build up, edify, and bring life and encouragement to those who hear them.

Prov. 10.11 – The mouth of the righteous is a fountain of life, but the mouth of the wicked conceals violence.

Prov. 16.21 – The wise of heart is called discerning, and sweetness of speech increases persuasiveness.

Prov. 16.23-24 - The heart of the wise makes his speech judicious and adds persuasiveness to his lips. [24] Gracious words are like a honeycomb, sweetness to the soul and health to the body.

Prov. 25.12 – Like a gold ring or an ornament of gold is a wise reprover to a listening ear.

Isa. 50.4 – The Lord GOD has given me the tongue of those who are taught, that I may know how to sustain with a word him who is weary. Morning by morning he awakens; he awakens my ear to hear as those who are taught.

Eph. 4.29 – Let no corrupting talk come out of your mouths, but only such as is good for building up, as fits the occasion, that it may give grace to those who hear.

Appropriate words are spoken at the right time, in the right way, and at the right place

Eccles. 3.1-8 – For everything there is a season, and a time for every matter under heaven: [2] a time to be born, and a time to die; a time to plant, and a time to pluck up what is planted; [3] a time to kill, and a time to heal; a time to break down, and a time to build up; [4] a time to weep, and a time to laugh; a time to mourn, and a time to dance; [5] a time to cast away stones, and a time to gather stones together; a time to embrace, and a time to refrain from embracing; [6] a time to seek, and a time to lose; a time to keep, and a time to cast away; [7] a time to tear, and a time to sew; a time to keep silence, and a time to speak; [8] a time to love, and a time to hate; a time for war, and a time for peace.

Prov. 15.23 – To make an apt answer is a joy to a man, and a word in season, how good it is!

Prov. 15.28 The heart of the righteous ponders how to answer, but the mouth of the wicked pours out evil things.

Prov. 25.11-12 – A word fitly spoken is like apples of gold in a setting of silver. [12] Like a gold ring or an ornament of gold is a wise reprover to a listening ear.

Silence and restraint in use of words displays wisdom and provides many benefits

Prov. 11.12-13 – Whoever belittles his neighbor lacks sense, but a man of understanding remains silent. [13] Whoever goes about slandering reveals secrets, but he who is trustworthy in spirit keeps a thing covered.

Prov. 10.19 – When words are many, transgression is not lacking, but whoever restrains his lips is prudent.

Prov. 17.27-28 – Whoever restrains his words has knowledge, and he who has a cool spirit is a man of understanding. [28] Even a fool who keeps silent is considered wise; when he closes his lips, he is deemed intelligent.

Prov. 21.23 – Whoever keeps his mouth and his tongue keeps himself out of trouble.

Prov. 26.4 – Answer not a fool according to his folly, lest you be like him yourself.

Eccles. 5.2-3 – Be not rash with your mouth, nor let your heart be hasty to utter a word before God, for God is in heaven and you are on earth. Therefore let your words be few. [3] For a dream comes with much business, and a fool's voice with many words.

Amos 5.13 – Therefore he who is prudent will keep silent in such a time, for it is an evil time.

Hab. 2.20 – But the LORD is in his holy temple; let all the earth keep silence before him.

Zeph. 1.7 – Be silent before the Lord GOD! For the day of the LORD is near; the LORD has prepared a sacrifice and consecrated his guests.

James 1.19 – Know this, my beloved brothers: let every person be quick to hear, slow to speak, slow to anger

Speak words that strengthen faith and make the truth of the Gospel clear to those who hear

Rom. 10.17 – So faith comes from hearing, and hearing through the word of Christ.

Isa. 50.4 – The Lord GOD has given me the tongue of those who are taught, that I may know how to sustain with a word him who is weary. Morning by morning he awakens; he awakens my ear to hear as those who are taught.

Acts 2.40-41 – And with many other words he bore witness and continued to exhort them, saying, "Save yourselves from this crooked generation." [41] So those who received his word were baptized, and there were added that day about three thousand souls.

Acts 28.23-24 – When they had appointed a day for him, they came to him at his lodging in greater numbers. From morning till evening he expounded to them, testifying to the kingdom of God and trying to convince them about Jesus both from the Law of Moses and from the Prophets. [24] And some were convinced by what he said, but others disbelieved.

1 Pet. 3.15-16 – but in your hearts honor Christ the Lord as holy, always being prepared to make a defense to anyone who asks you for a reason for the hope that is in you; yet do it with gentleness and respect, [16] having a good conscience, so that, when you are slandered, those who revile your good behavior in Christ may be put to shame.

The Cycle of Selfish Preoccupation: Representation Gone Sour

Rev. Dr. Don L. Davis

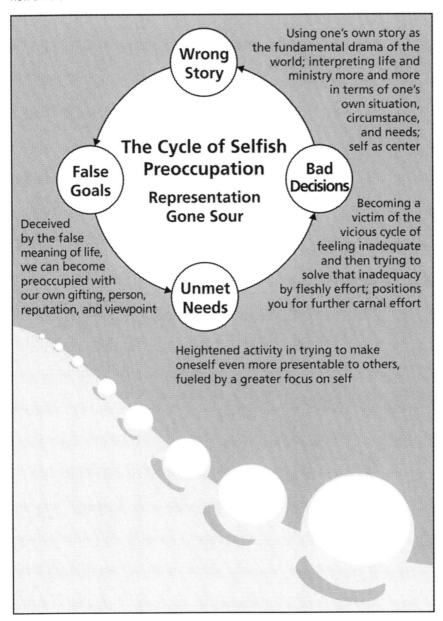

Wrong Story

Using one's own story as the fundamental drama of the world; interpreting life and ministry more and more in terms of one's own situation, circumstance, and needs; self as center

The Cycle of Selfish Preoccupation

Representation Gone Sour

False Goals

Bad Decisions

Deceived by the false meaning of life, we can become preoccupied with our own gifting, person, reputation, and viewpoint

Becoming a victim of the vicious cycle of feeling inadequate and then trying to solve that inadequacy by fleshly effort; positions you for further carnal effort

Unmet Needs

Heightened activity in trying to make oneself even more presentable to others, fueled by a greater focus on self

Discerning Root Issues

Rev. Dr. Don L. Davis

Discerning and addressing the root issues is key to all pastoral care

1 Thess. 5.14-15 – And we urge you, brothers, admonish the idle, encourage the fainthearted, help the weak, be patient with them all. [15] See that no one repays anyone evil for evil, but always seek to do good to one another and to everyone.

Admonish *the idle*

Encourage *THE FAINTHEARTED*

Help the weak

Be patient **WITH ALL**

Repay evil TO NONE

Do good to one another and to everyone

From Deep Ignorance to Credible Witness

Rev. Dr. Don L. Davis

Witness - Ability to give witness and teach
2 Tim. 2.2
Matt. 28.18-20
1 John 1.1-4
Prov. 20.6
2 Cor. 5.18-21

And the things you have heard me say in the presence of many witnesses entrust to reliable men who will also be qualified to teach others.
~ 2 Tim. 2.2

8

Lifestyle - Consistent appropriation and habitual practice based on beliefs
Heb. 5.11-6.2
Eph. 4.11-16
2 Pet. 3.18
1 Tim. 4.7-10

And Jesus increased in wisdom and in stature, and in favor with God and man.
~ Luke 2.52

7

Demonstration - Expressing conviction in corresponding conduct, speech, and behavior
James 2.14-26
2 Cor. 4.13
2 Pet. 1.5-9
1 Thess. 1.3-10

Nevertheless, at your word I will let down the net.
~ Luke 5.5

6

Conviction - Committing oneself to think, speak, and act in light of information
Heb. 2.3-4
Heb. 11.1, 6
Heb. 3.15-19
Heb. 4.2-6

Do you believe this?
~ John 11.26

5

Discernment - Understanding the meaning and implications of information
John 16.13
Eph. 1.15-18
Col. 1.9-10
Isa. 6.10; 29.10

Do you understand what you are reading?
~ Acts 8.30

4

Knowledge - Ability to recall and recite information
2 Tim. 3.16-17
1 Cor. 2.9-16
1 John 2.20-27
John 14.26

For what does the Scripture say?
~ Rom. 4.3

3

Interest - Responding to ideas or information with both curiosity and openness
Ps. 42.1-2
Acts 9.4-5
John 12.21
1 Sam. 3.4-10

We will hear you again on this matter.
~ Acts 17.32

2

Awareness - General exposure to ideas and information
Mark 7.6-8
Acts 19.1-7
John 5.39-40
Matt. 7.21-23

At that time, Herod the tetrarch heard about the fame of Jesus.
~ Matt. 14.1

1

Ignorance - Unfamiliarity with information due to naivete, indifference, or hardness
Eph. 4.17-19
Ps. 2.1-3
Rom. 1.21; 2.19
1 John 2.11

Who is the Lord that I should heed his voice?
~ Exod. 5.2

0

Toward a Hermeneutic of Critical Engagement

Rev. Dr. Don L. Davis

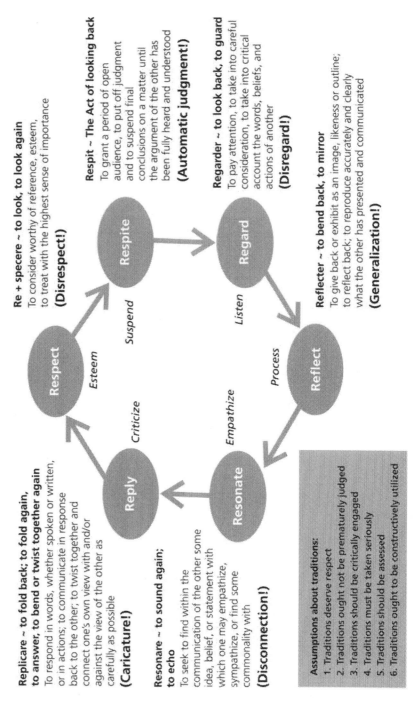

Re + specere ~ to look, to look again
To consider worthy of reference, esteem, to treat with the highest sense of importance
(Disrespect!)

Respit ~ The Act of looking back
To grant a period of open audience, to put off judgment and to suspend final conclusions on a matter until the argument of the other has been fully heard and understood
(Automatic judgment!)

Regarder ~ to look back, to guard
To pay attention, to take into careful consideration, to take into critical account the words, beliefs, and actions of another
(Disregard!)

Reflecter ~ to bend back, to mirror
To give back or exhibit as an image, likeness or outline; to reflect back; to reproduce accurately and clearly what the other has presented and communicated
(Generalization!)

Replicare ~ to fold back; to fold again, to answer, to bend or twist together again
To respond in words, whether spoken or written, or in actions; to communicate in response back to the other; to twist together and connect one's own view with and/or against the view of the other as carefully as possible
(Caricature!)

Resonare ~ to sound again; to echo
To seek to find within the communication of the other some idea, belief, or statement with which one may empathize, sympathize, or find some commonality with
(Disconnection!)

Respect — Esteem — Suspend — Respite — Listen — Regard — Process — Reflect — Empathize — Resonate — Criticize — Reply

Assumptions about traditions:
1. Traditions deserve respect
2. Traditions ought not be prematurely judged
3. Traditions should be critically engaged
4. Traditions must be taken seriously
5. Traditions should be assessed
6. Traditions ought to be constructively utilized

The Way of Wisdom

Rev. Dr. Don L. Davis

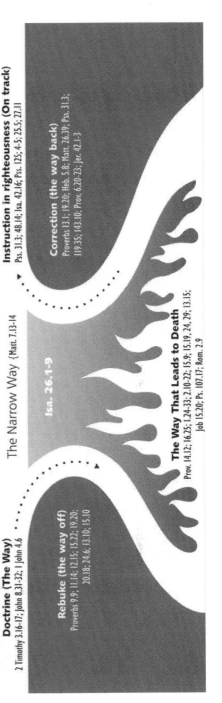

Sowing and Reaping {Gal. 6.7-8}

You will **sow**

You will **reap** what you sow

You will reap **more than** what you sow

You will reap in **proportion** to what you sow

You will reap **in kind** as you sow

You will reap in a **different season** than you sow

You determine what you sow

You can **sow differently** than you did last year

You reap more if you **cultivate and fertilize**

Your sowing can **affect what others reap** also

What you **think about**

How you **dress**

How you **speak**

Who you **hang out with**

What you **listen to and look at**

What you **read**

Where you **go**

How you **make decisions**

What your **goals** are

What's important to you

The Goal

Be like Jesus
1 Cor. 11.2; Rom. 8.29; Phil. 3.8-12

Loving God with all our heart
Deut. 6.4-6; Matt. 22.34-40

Loving our neighbors as ourselves
Lev 19.18; Matt. 7.12

The Way of Life { Proverbs 1.7-8; 4.13; 8.10; 9.9; 10.17; 13.18; 15.32-33; 23.23 }

The Narrow Way {Matt. 7.13-14}

Isa. 26.1-9

Instruction in righteousness (On track)
Pss. 31.3; 48.14; Isa. 42.16; Pss. 125; 4-5; 25.5; 27.11

Correction (the way back)
Proverbs 13.1; 19.20; Heb. 5.8; Matt. 26.39; Pss. 31.3; 119.35; 143.10; Prov. 6.20-23; Jer. 42.1-3

Doctrine (The Way)
2 Timothy 3.16-17; John 8.31-32; 1 John 4.6

Rebuke (the way off)
Proverbs 9.9; 11.14; 12.15; 15.22; 19.20; 20.18; 24.6; 13.10; 15.10

The Way That Leads to Death
Prov. 14.12; 16.25; 1.24-33; 2.10-22; 15.9; 15.19, 24, 29; 13.15; Job 15.20; Ps. 107.17; Rom. 2.9

Boiling Down to the One

Rev. Dr. Don L. Davis

	One Thing I Desire, Ps. 27.4-5	One Thing Is Needful, Luke 10.38-42	This One Thing I Do, Phil. 3.12-14
Meaning of the One	The Godly disciple of Jesus boils down his or her desire to a single passion for the Lord God himself	The godly disciple of Jesus understands life through the lens of the Kingdom of God, Matt. 6.33	The godly disciple of Jesus evaluates all activities in light of what has eternal significance, 2 Cor. 4.18-19
Area of Concern	The priority of your *passions* (THE POWER OF SPIRITUAL DESIRE)	The priority of your *perspective*	The priority of your *practice*
The Challenge of Multiplicity	*Many desires unleashed and unchecked* make everything you want equally satisfying and fulfilling, James 1.5	*Many perspectives unanalyzed* make everything appear necessary and believable, Eph. 4.11-15; 1 Cor. 2; 2 Cor. 10.3-5	*Many practices unevaluated and unweighed* make everything you do equally important and urgent, 1 Cor. 3.9-15
Why This Is Critical	1. Your desires are many and tend to cause dissatisfaction ("I can't get no satisfaction, but I try!" - Rolling Stones), Prov. 27.20 2. You are tempted by runaway and unchecked desire, James 1.13-14	1. We are prone to believe anything and everything that makes our lives more comfortable and consistent with the way of our flesh, Gal. 5.16-24 2. You are blown about by every wind of doctrine which tells you how important, necessary, and urgent some idea or item is, when in fact it is not, Matt. 16.24-26	1. We ignore God's invitations to grow and to give while squandering our time on things that we like, not on things that are of ultimate concern, Matt. 22.1-14 2. We will have no fruit of our lives, living only for temporal things of marginal importance, 1 Cor. 3.9-15
The Danger of Ignoring This Principle	*Victim of unclear, hobo desires* (wandering, constant burden to follow every passion you have)	*Victim of becoming an intellectual groupie* (attaching yourself to the latest fad of thinking and not the Word of God) SOMEBODY IS GONNA MOVE	*Victim of living a shotgun lifestyle* (living scattered, unfocused, non-targeted, being involved in things that aim but without focus or clarity)
Practical Implication	Your passions must be *guarded and educated* or you will be consumed by your own desires	Your perspectives must be *renewed by the Word of God* or you will be bamboozled by the lies and perspectives of the world, Rom. 12.1-2	Your practices must be *weighed against kingdom values*, or you will make convincing excuses to yourself for why you cannot participate in the very work of the living God to reconciles the world to himself, 2 Cor. 5.18-21
Helpful Illustration	DESPERATE ENOUGH TO FIND GOD OVERDEPENDENCE ON OTHERS	HOW TO BE COMPLETELY GULLIBLE	WHEN CLOSE ENOUGH IS ENOUGH RUNNING FOR YOUR LIFE
Proverb	Where your treasure is, there will your heart be also. Guard your heart with all diligence, for out of it comes forth the issues of life	You live your life not on the basis of what is necessary, but what you think is necessary to you	The genius of a life well lived is understanding that only a few things really matter. Concentrate on them.
What You Must Do	Ask God to turn your heart to your love for Christ, his body, and his Kingdom DON'T LIVE HALFHEARTEDLY	Begin to renew your mind again by abiding in the Word of Jesus, John 8.31-32	Redo your schedule with Christ and his Kingdom as your ultimate priority ARE THERE ANY MEN OF GOD

Substitute Centers to a Christ-Centered Vision:
Goods and Effects Which Our Culture Substitutes as the Ultimate Concern

Rev. Dr. Don L. Davis

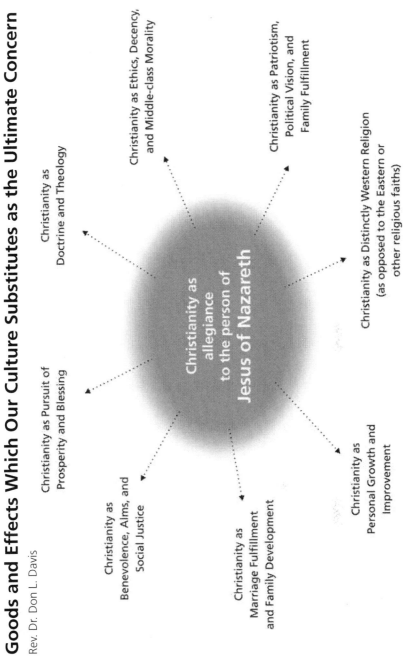

Christianity as
Doctrine and Theology

Christianity as Ethics, Decency,
and Middle-class Morality

Christianity as Patriotism,
Political Vision, and
Family Fulfillment

Christianity as Pursuit of
Prosperity and Blessing

Christianity as allegiance
to the person of
Jesus of Nazareth

Christianity as Distinctly Western Religion
(as opposed to the Eastern or
other religious faiths)

Christianity as
Benevolence, Alms, and
Social Justice

Christianity as
Marriage Fulfillment
and Family Development

Christianity as
Personal Growth and
Improvement

The Importance of Discipline
Rev. Dr. Don L. Davis

Discipline is what moderns need the most and want the least.

Too often young people who leave home, students who quit
school, husbands and wives who seek divorce, church members
who neglect services, employees who walk out on their jobs are
simply trying to escape discipline. The true motive may often be
camouflaged by a hundred excuses, but behind the flimsy front
is the hard core of aversion to restraint and control.

Much of our restlessness and instability can be traced to this basic
fault in modern character. Our overflowing asylums and hospitals
and jails are but symptoms of an undisciplined age. There may
be many secondary causes and there may be many secondary
cures, but somewhere behind them all is the need for discipline.
The kind of discipline needed is far deeper than the rule of alarm
clocks and time cards; it embraces self-restraint, courage,
perseverance, and resiliency as the inner panoply of the soul.

Many nervous and emotional disorders are the accumulated
result of years of self-indulgent living. I am not thinking of the
drunkards or the libertines, but of the respectable Christians
who probably would be horrified at the thought of touching
liquor or indulging in gross immorality. But they are nevertheless
undisciplined, and the fatal weakness is unmasked in the day
of trial and adversity. A lifelong pattern of running away from
difficulties, of avoiding incompatible people, of seeking the
easy way, of quitting when the going gets rough finally shows
up in a neurotic semi-invalidism and incapacity. Numerous
books may be read, many doctors and preachers consulted,
innumerable prayers may be offered, and religious commitments

made; the patient may be inundated with drugs, advice, costly treatment, and spiritual scourgings; yet none lay bare the real cause: lack of discipline. And the only real cure is to become a disciplined person.

~ Richard Shelly Taylor. *The Disciplined Life.*
Kansas City: Beacon Hill Press, 1962. pp. 10-11

Key questions for understanding the role of discipline in God's call to holiness

1. Is *discipline* the same as *holiness?*

2. Are there any cases where discipline can become a *substitute* for holiness?

3. Can *discipline* bring about or produce *holiness?*

4. If *discipline* does not produce *holiness,* then what are the benefits of discipline for us?

5. For growing Christians and ministers, what is the most biblical way to understand the relationship of *discipline* to *holiness?*

Made in the USA
Columbia, SC
26 May 2018